GG's Home for The Holidays COOKBOOK

Alveda C. King
With Jan Horne

STANTON
PUBLISHING HOUSE

GG's HOME FOR THE HOLIDAYS COOKSOOK

Stanton Publishing House

3355 Lenox Rd Suite 750

ATLANTA, GA 30326

www.stantonpublishinghosue.com

Professional video footage courtesy of studio25production and CBN television,

Recipes, photos of recipes and home videos by Alveda C. King

ISBN 978-0-9992795-5-7

www.alvedaking.com

Contents

Video QR Codes

Tips & Notes

GG's Opening Tidbits

Hello. I'm Evangelist Alveda (GG, Gorgeous Grandma) King. For seven generations members of the Williams-King Family Legacy, the family of Martin Luther King, Sr. and his wife Alberta Williams King, have been preaching and cooking, providing ministry and hospitality in the midst of tragedy and triumph, trials and victories. This book is a collection of the memories of those times blended in with favorite holiday recipes inspired by family members and friends. As far as organization of the meals, menus and dishes goes, look for a "flow" among holiday themes, with mementoes and notes tucked in between the bites. **Get free QR codes app and scan for video recipe demonstrations.**

This is a "gluten friendly" homemade cookbook featuring homemade meals. However, any of the recipes can be customized with various types of flour and other ingredients which suit the palates of the cooks. Also, for those who shy away from "night shades" such as tomatoes, bell peppers and eggplant, you will discover alternative dishes herein. While turkey is featured as a star protein in the book, any of the poultry dishes can be prepared with chicken as well, allowing you to choose your protein. And there are "veggie" choices tucked in too.

My friend Jan Horne is an incredible videographer, so look for her clips along with some "home video" You Tube clips from "yours truly". From our hearts to yours, from our home test kitchens to your tables, we pray that you will enjoy this collection of food, fun, love and fellowship with us.

KING FAMILY LEGACY
HOLIDAY FLAVORS
FAVORITE HOLIDAY RECIPES
SEASONED WITH LOVE

KITCHEN BLESSINGS FOR COOKS AND EATERS

1. A praying family who eats together stays together.
2. Love is the key ingredient in every meal.
3. Don't cook when you are angry, hungry or in a hurry.
4. Invest in good spices. Try a deck or window herb garden.
5. Keep a well stocked pantry; quality dry and canned goods.
6. Once a week (at least) sit down and eat together.
7. Clean out the fridge weekly; reinvent leftovers.
8. Turn off the media when you have a family sit down meal.
9. Cook together, food shop together, eat together.
10. Clean up the kitchen together.
11. If you don't cook, keep the cook company in the kitchen.
12. Every home chef loves a good souse chef.

Tools of the Trade

My mother Naomi has always been a source of insight and inspiration when it comes to navigating this journey called life. For instance, she has insisted that I have what she calls "car pride and pot pride." This attitude is best described as having a visible appreciation for the care and maintenance of one's cars and one's pots and pans in the kitchen. Through the years, when Mother rides in my car, she expects it to be "clean as a whistle." Never mind the constant stream of children and now grandchildren GG has to feed and transport. "A good Christian is an organized, neat and clean Christian," says Nonnie. Over the years I have amassed a pretty good set of kitchen tools, many of which you see in my home videos in our family kitchen at home. The QR Codes are Jan's idea. This process of collecting and publishing recipes using home kitchen tools and inventory has been a monumental task that is well worth the effort. Our Sunday Suppers have been our "test kitchen," where we have applied our skills and tools to the task of delivering love in the form of food to our readers and viewers. We have used everything at hand to get this done. We all have our cherished culinary investments; a favorite pot, our gently worn apron, our expensive food processor... What's in your arsenal?

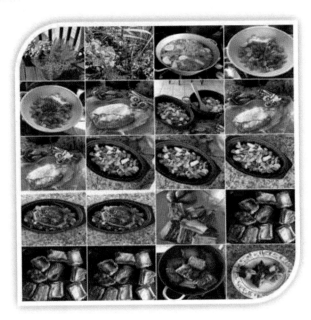

Over a period of time, we cooks tend to gather favorite herbs and spices. Regional and cultural tastes should dictate your collection. For fun, try buying a new spice or herb monthly. Some staples should be found in every kitchen. To name a few:

From the Herb Garden

Rosemary
Basil
Chives
Oregano
Thyme
Lemon Grass
Sage
Parsley

From the Pantry and Frig

Sea Salt
Red, White and Black Pepper
Paprika (Smoked)
Lemons
Potatoes
Onions
Celery
Assorted Brown Sauces
Mayo
Butter
Assorted Cooking Oils
Assorted Spices and Extracts

GG's Porch and Pantry Notes

A well stocked pantry and herb garden can save you money and time. Shopping in bulk for spices and seasonings and growing herbs in your kitchen window, or outside on your deck or in your yard can be fun and rewarding.

"Thank you for reading our book. We pray that you will be blessed as you share our meals with friends and family."

Alveda (GG) King
and
Jan (Studio 25) Horne

"All of this is for your benefit. And as God's grace reaches more and more people, there will be great thanksgiving, and God will receive more and more glory."
2 Corinthians 4:15 NLT

The Birth of the Sunday Supper Test Kitchen

Hot on the heels of the decision to accept the suggestion of a favorite Christian television show producer which was to write this cookbook, the realization that if this was to happen I would have to draw upon the discipline not only for cooking, I would have to write and test the recipes. I had been toying with the cookbook idea for a few years, but had yet to make a commitment.

In 2016, after consulting with Jan and agreeing that we would use our new "Home for The Holidays" video project as a base for the cookbook, I began to record recipes and cook the dishes. Because I am a "shake and pour cook" in the style of my mother, this was no easy task. I was so used to cooking by mood and inspiration that I found it a challenge to cook the same dish twice. I was used to adding a different dash here and a new pinch there. It became a family joke. "Make her write it down."

During this same season the political climate was heating up. Families began to feud over their choices of candidates for the upcoming U.S. presidential election. Meanwhile, Jan would call every few weeks to ask how the project was coming. I was finally compiling the recipes and fine tuning some dishes. As the 2016 Thanksgiving and Christmas Holiday season approached, I opened my home and my kitchen for "Sunday Supper" in the tradition of Williams-King suppers from years gone by. I was determined that there would be "no ripping turkey legs off and beating people over the head with them" in political fury. We would love each other. As friends and family, we would fellowship together, break bread over Sunday Supper, and test GG's recipes. The culmination of these encounters has resulted in this cookbook. It has been a blessed and tasty journey.

In 1950, Rev. Alfred Daniel Williams King married Naomi Ruth Barber. They moved into what is now the historic "King Family Birth Home" which is in Atlanta, Georgia.

As members of "The Martin Luther King Family," A. D. and Naomi were the first in their generation to marry and raise a family. Rev. Martin Luther King, Sr. and his beloved wife Mrs. Alberta Williams King [Daddy King and Mama King] are the original patriarch and matriarch of the "King Family Legacy."

Rev. Dr. Martin Luther King, Jr. married Coretta Scott and became the most famous member of this historic family. Sister Christine King married Mr. Isaac Farris, Sr. and they helped to build the MLK Center. The rest is history. Yet there is one little known grace upon our family:

Home for The Holidays Family Tradition

King Family Legacy Thanksgiving 1963

Young AD King Family At Home

While the members of our historic "King Family Legacy" are noted for our leadership in the Christian Church and in The Civil Rights Movement of the 20th century, our legendary culinary skills and gifts of hospitality have been a best kept secret for far too long.

So please enjoy this cookbook from the family of Rev. A. D. and Mrs. Naomi King; may our faith in God, Agape Love and culinary delights add joy to your souls and bless your tables.

Now and Then

"Back Then" the dinner table was set every day; the family waited for "Dad" to come home from work; scriptures were quoted, prayers of thanksgiving were raised; and the family conversed over tasty meals. Problems of the world were solved and blessings abounded.

GG's 21st Century Kitchen

King Family Birth Home 20th Century Kitchen

The world moves faster today; not much time for daily meal gathering; we try hard during the week and make Sunday Suppers our priority quality time.

Turkey Too!

Of course Thanksgiving is a favorite season which is always complete with a lovely roasted turkey. Pictured here is our traditional roasted turkey. We usually add a smoked turkey to the table as well. This usually leaves plenty of leftovers for our day after turkey soup and turkey salad.

GG's Turkey Soup

Basic Ingredients

2 -3 cups Chopped leftover
   turkey
4 stalks celery
2 quarts water or turkey broth
1 large chopped onion
Cup chopped carrots
1 cup brown rice or 4 oz.
   noodles
Stalk fresh rosemary
Pinch of nutmeg
Sea Salt to taste

Add all ingredients to large pot. Bring to boil then reduce to simmer for 30 minutes. Dish up and enjoy!

GG's Day After Turkey Salad

Basic Ingredients

3 cups Chopped Turkey Breast
3 stalks chopped celery
3 boiled eggs
1 cup mayonnaise
1 teaspoon mustard
Pinch of dried dill
Sea Salt to taste

Chop turkey and put into a mixing bowl. Add chopped celery, mayonnaise, chopped eggs, mustard, dill and salt. Mix well and refrigerate until ready to serve. Plate and enjoy!

 **GG's Favorite Sunday Supper
(Great for Holidays too!)**

Seasoned With Love

Sunday Supper is a King Family Tradition that we enjoy keeping in our busy lives. Family dinners around the table are a wonderful way to strengthen the love, character and values of the family unit. Through the years, our family cooks have brought many memorable dishes such as Aunt Christine's famous fried chicken, Aunt Coretta's unforgettable vegetable soup, Big Mama's Delmonico steaks and so much more. This tradition of Sunday Supper remains with us today.

Often on Sunday mornings, GG (Gorgeous Grandma) rises early, and after moments of prayer and reflection over the blessings in the lives of her family, she slips to the kitchen while everyone is still sleeping and prepares the meal which will be savored after church. Don't let the pinches and dashes fluster you; they just indicate season to taste.

Menu
Southern Style Turkey Cutlets, Sautéed Garlicky Green Beans, Yummy Gluten Free Cornbread Stuffing, Leafy Salad, Sparkling Water with Lemon, Vanilla Ice Cream with Chocolate Syrup and Fresh Strawberries (Meal for four)

GG's Southern Style Turkey Cutlets

1 pound fresh turkey cutlets
½ Cup Rice Flour
2 tbs. minced onion
1 tbs. chopped garlic
2 tbs. fresh rosemary leaves
Pinch cayenne pepper
Pinch Pink Himalayan Sea Salt
1 tbs. butter
2 tbs. Olive or Coconut oil
1 cup turkey broth

Optional ingredients and preparations: This recipe works well with chicken and pork. Adding your favorite hot wing sauce brings a spicy buffalo cutlet option to the table.

Pour rice flour into a shaker bag; add pinch of salt and pinch of cayenne pepper. Shake bag to mix dry ingredients. Rinse and add turkey cutlets to bag. The rinse adds moisture to help flour cling to cutlets. Shake the bag with dry mix and turkey until turkey is well dusted. Turn on a skillet and add oil. Heat until oil is hot. Add turkey, brown on both sides. Pour in turkey broth and sprinkle minced onions, garlic and rosemary over cutlets. Reduce heat and simmer for 10 minutes. Let rest until time plating and then spoon reduction of broth onto plate and place cutlet over reduction. Add a rosemary garnish if desired. Enjoy!

Broiled Fish
Tasty Gifts from the Sea

Of course fried fish is often "all the rage." Still, there's a lot to be said about a really well prepared broiled fillet of your favorite taste of the sea. Pictured here are salmon and trout. However, this recipe works with most selections.

Ingredients

2 pounds of fish fillets
¼ cup olive oil
Olive oil spray
½ stick of butter
¼ cup lemon juice
1 stalk fresh rosemary
Dash of seafood seasoning
Sea salt to taste
Blended pepper (optional)
Capers (optional)
Dash Garlic Powder
Dash Onion Powder
Dash Smokey Paprika

Preheat oven to 450 degrees. Rinse fish and pat dry. Cover bottom of baking pan with olive oil Sprinkle half of dry ingredients over oil. Place fish onto seasoned oil. Spray with olive oil and sprinkle with remaining dry ingredients. Drizzle with lemon juice, add pats of butter and rosemary sprigs. Cook until flaky yet moist. (About ten minutes) Serve with sides and/or salad. Enjoy!

Stunning Savory Holiday Roasts

The secret to a successful roast is in finding the perfect balance, marinade, cooking time and temperature. While some diners prefer a warm pink center and others enjoy well done cut of flavor, the cook wants to deliver something satisfying to the plate.

Basic Ingredients

3-4 pound Prime Roast Cut of Lamb, Pork or Beef
1 cup olive oil
¼ cup sea salt
¼ cup coarse garlic powder
¼ cup onion powder
1 tbs. smoked paprika
2 tbs. minced rosemary
1/3 cup garlic cloves
Dash Nutmeg
Dash of Blended Pepper (optional)

Make every recipe your own by adding your favorite herb and spices

The first step is the marinade which works best when applied at least four hours before cook time. Place the roast in pan or covered bowl. Cover with the olive oil. Add the dry ingredients, distributing evenly throughout. Cover until ready for oven. Preheat oven to 475 degrees. Pierce very small slices in the roast and insert the garlic buds. (Some cooks prefer to sear roast in a pan instead of this next step). Place the roast in appropriate roasting pan into the oven until the surface is brown. Once the roast is browned and the spices and herbs have formed a crust on the roast lower the temperature to 425 degrees until roast reaches the desired temperature. Test with a meat thermometer. Remove from oven. Rest and serve. Enjoy!

Festive Holiday Dishes

Christmas carols, Holiday Cookies, Blueberry Bread, and Tea by the fire, (with a few chestnuts roasting) from our house to yours. Our quick and easy Blueberry Bread is our secret (we use any box mix), add a pinch of orange zest, a pat of butter a smidgen of nutmeg and a dash of vanilla.

Comfort and Joy

"Take a Break"
What can be more Comforting during the holidays, and indeed anytime, than a bowl of warm and hearty soup, a hug and a prayer?

GG's Lovely Lunch Break

GG's Turkey Swedish Meatballs

Ingredients
1 lb ground turkey
¼ cup minced onions
1 tbs garlic powder
¼ cup plain yogurt
½ cup olive oil
1 tsp salt
1 tsp pepper
1 tbs olive oil

Heat skillet while shaping turkey into meatballs. Drop the meatballs into pan, cook while turning to brown evenly. Serve over a dressed salad with a side of steamed or baked spaghetti squash. (A nice vegetarian meatball is a lovely and delicious alternative.) Enjoy!

Leafy Salad with Berries or Tomatoes

Fresh salad greens come in many varieties these days. Arugula is popular. Watercress is tasty. The secret to good salad is texture and color. For those who shy away from tomatoes, strawberries, blackberries, blueberries or raspberries are delicious in season. Pick a bag or try your own. Enjoy!

GG's Sautéed Garlicky Green Beans

Ingredients
16 oz. fresh green beans, whole
¼ cup chopped garlic
¼ cup olive oil
Pinch Pink Himalayan Sea Salt

This popular side dish is colorful, delicious and quick and easy.
Simply heat a frying pan, pour in olive oil, add green beans, salt and
garlic and stir as the beans cook for about four minutes. Allow to
become tender, but not soggy. Ready, set, yummy. Enjoy!

GG's Yummy Gluten Free Holiday Cornbread Stuffing

2 cups Self Rising Gluten Free Cornmeal (or box of
    gluten free cornbread mix)
1 cup buttermilk
2 eggs
3/4 cup olive oil
½ stick butter
Pinch of Himalayan Sea Salt
3 stalks celery chopped finely
½ Bell Pepper chopped finely
¾ cups golden raisins
½ teaspoon nutmeg
2 tbs. fresh rosemary leaves
3 tbs. fresh sage, chopped
2 cups turkey broth

Preheat oven to 375 degrees. Add butter to 8x8x2 inches baking pan.
When oven is hot, put the pan in the oven to melt butter while
preparing the stuffing. Bake the cornbread mix as directed on package,
or make the cornbread in a pan after mixing cornmeal, eggs,
buttermilk, salt and ½ cup olive oil before preparing the stuffing. Once
the cornbread is ready with a brown crust, crumble the cornbread in a
large mixing bowl. Add the celery, bell pepper, raisins, nutmeg,
rosemary, sage, ¼ cup olive oil and turkey broth. Stir to mix well. Bake
in hot oven for 20 minutes or until brown. Serve with some of the
remaining gravy from the turkey. Enjoy!

We always make extra cornbread batter for muffins!

Known today as "The Butterfly Queen," this beautiful and gracious lady has weathered the trials and triumphs of two centuries. As the widow of slain 20th Century Civil Rights Activist Rev. AD King, Dr. Naomi King is a noted activist in her own rights. In her early days as First Lady of the churches where Her husband, Rev. A. D. King presided as Pastor, as well as a civil rights leader, Naomi presided as the "hostess with the mostess" inspiring many with her Hospitality and well set tables.

"Angel Eggs"

Basic Ingredients

1 dozen eggs	**Optional additions**
½ cup mayo	Bacon Bits
1/3 cup pickle relish	Crab
Salt to taste	Shredded Cheese
Dash Paprika	

Boil eggs in salted water for 3-4 minutes. Peel while warm. Cut eggs in half and remove yokes and place in a mixing bowl. Set egg whites on serving platter. Spoon remaining ingredients except paprika and parsley into bowl with the yokes. Blend by hand with a fork until mixture is smooth and creamy. Spoon into egg white caps. Garnish with paprika and parsley. Enjoy!

By day, Rev. Dr. Derek Barber King is a college professor, preacher and noted civil rights activist. In our home kitchen, "Chef Derek" reigns supreme. Drawing from his experiences growing up in the 20th Century Civil Rights era, where Derek learned to "pray, preach and cook from his parents Rev. A. D. and Mrs. Naomi King, Derek often delights our palates with plates inspired by kitchens from around the world. Watch his handy conch prep tips here.

Conch is a seafaring dish popular in the Caribbean Islands. While this versatile "staple of the sea" can be Prepared many ways (including fried, fritters and ceviche), this basic stew recipe is a great place to start.

GG's Conch Stew

Ingredients

2 pounds fresh shelled conch
1 quart turkey broth
¼ cup fresh chopped garlic
½ cup chopped onion
½ cup olive oil
Fresh parsley to taste
Sea Salt to taste
Red pepper to taste
¼ cup curry powder
½ cup chopped celery

Heat oven or crock pot to 350 degrees. Trim conch. Pound with meat mallet until tender. Rinse and place in roasting pan. Add other ingredients and cook in oven until conch is tender (about two hours). Serve over seasoned rice with steamed okra and fresh salad. Enjoy!

GG's Scallops and Grits

GG's variation of Shrimp and Grits uses pan seared scallops, stone ground grits, bacon, scallions (or chives), and fresh sweet (English) peas.

Ingredients

1 cup uncooked grits	1 cup of milk	1 tbs olive oil	bacon
1 lb scallops	1 tbs salt	¼ stick butter or substitute	
3 oz cream cheese	¼ cup chopped scallions or chives		
2 cups of water	1 cup steamed green peas		

Heat skillet while preparing grits. Bring water and milk to a boil in medium saucepan. Pour grits into boiling liquid and cook to desired consistency. Add salt. Stir in cream cheese. Lower heat. Sprinkle salt onto scallops. Add oil to skillet and drop scallops into pan. Brown evenly on each side. Stir grits as scallops are cooking. Spoon grits into bowl; top with scallops, add peas, sprinkle Scallions; add bacon and pat of butter. A lovely dish for brunch or hearty breakfast. Enjoy!

GG's Egg Soufflé

While I'm a big fan of quiche and frittatas, over the years, I've tried to "streamline" a few of my dishes. This crust free eggy pie is a popular show stopper as a covered dish item; I often make it for Church Socials. As a casserole, it works for breakfast, brunch and even dinner.

Ingredients

One dozen fresh eggs
One cup fat free half and half
¼ cup chopped celery
¼ cup chopped onions
¼ cup minced garlic
2 tsp. sea salt

¼ cup diced bell peppers (optional)
1 sprig of chopped rosemary
¼ cup olive oil
¼ cup diced protein (bacon, turkey, ham, etc.)
2 cups shredded cheese (your choice)

Preheat oven to 425 degrees. Crack eggs and pour into a mixing bowl. Stir until yokes and whites are blended. Stir in half and half. Add remaining ingredients. Stir until well blended. Pour into a baking dish. Bake until the dish "sets" and rises into a puffy "soufflé." Remove from oven. Cool slightly and serve. Enjoy!

GG's Shirred Eggs
(Oeufs en Cocotte)

Baked eggs are different from poached eggs, in that the eggs are baked rather than boiled. This versatile recipe is great for breakfast and brunch times. Customize the dish with additions of your creative ingredients. This dish makes a pretty addition to your holiday table.

Basic Ingredients

1 dozen eggs
¼ cup chopped chives
½ cup shredded parmesan cheese
½ cup fat free half and half
1 stalk fresh rosemary
½ stick butter
2 tsp. sea salt
Dash of smoked paprika

Preheat oven to 350 degrees. Melt the butter in a baking pan, or in six ramakins. Remove from oven. Crack the eggs and pour into the baking pan or two per ramakin with the melted butter. Gently pour the half and half over the eggs. Sprinkle salt, cheese, chives and paprika over the eggs. Bake to desired doneness (5-7 minutes). Remove from oven. Brown the dish with a blow torch or under a broiler to melt cheese. Garnish with rosemary leaves, serve with a green salad and or fresh fruit. Enjoy!

Father and Son Barbecue Ribs

Rev. Derek King
Chef Derek King

Chef Derek's
Sweet and Spicy Rib Rub

Ingredients
2 cup brown sugar
2 tbsp cayenne pepper
1 t salt
2 tbsp garlic powder
1 t black pepper
.5 cup chili powder
.5 cup paprika
2 t celery salt
1 t allspice
1 t cinnamon

10 pounds pork spare ribs or baby back ribs

Combine dry ingredients for rub, sprinkle liberally and thoroughly, to evenly cover 10 pounds of pork ribs on both sides. Once covered, place ribs meat side down over flame. Let the ribs smoke for 1 hour at 225-275 degrees then flip meat and cook the other side for 1 hour.

After 2 hours remove meat from smoker place in an aluminum pan and seal tightly. Place the pan in a 250 degree oven and cook for an additional 2 hours. After 2 hours remove pan from oven and remove the lip from the pan. The ribs will be fork tender and the meat will pull away from the bone. Enjoy!

**King Family Legacy
Grill Masters
Tradition**

During the 20th century, holiday cookouts and grill skills were a King Family Tradition.

During the height of the Civil Rights Movement, with the ups and downs and life in the crosshairs, we family delighted in family gatherings, where Daddy thrilled our taste buds with ribs, steaks, sausages, fish, chicken, burgers and franks from his built-in smoke pit from our backyard. "Uncle" Isaac Farris, Sr. was also a prime grill master.

The legacy continues here in the 21st century with the Ellis family, and father and son duo Rev. Derek King and Chef Derek King. Hot off the grill and fresh to the table recipes can now be available for your family at thekingstable.com.

Family Favorites

Every family has its favorite dishes. Ours is no exception. Often people ask: "What was Martin Luther King's favorite food? As what is now legend has it, he really enjoyed fried chicken and collard greens. Here's an anecdote his sister-in-law, my mother Naomi shares from time to time:

Uncle ML had been stabbed in his chest during a ministry tour in New York with Dr. Billy Graham in 1958. He was also there for a book signing in Harlem, and was stabbed in the chest by a deranged woman. After being rushed to the hospital where his doctor told him: "Dr. King, if you had sneezed, you would have died." Well, my mother told him in a phone conversation as he was convalescing, "ML, I'm so glad you didn't sneeze." Mother's sentiments were echoed by a little elementary school girl who wrote him a get well note. Mother recalls that when Uncle ML was in the hospital, his wife Aunt Coretta flew up to visit him. Mother baked one of her "family famous" sweet potato cobblers and sent it along straight out of her oven with her best wishes. The pie was still warm from the oven and was well received by the patient.

Daddy was famous for bringing road weary civil rights warriors home to Mother's kitchen at all hours of the day and night. In those days, restaurants that served "Negroes" were few and far between, so the "foot soldiers" were always welcome in our home. Daddy especially loved breakfast foods, including luscious cheese and eggs, and Mother's breakfast sandwiches. Also, because Daddy was a world traveler, he introduced us to sumptuous dishes from around the world.

Granddaddy really enjoyed Aunt Coretta's corn bread with vegetable beef soup which was chocked full of okra, corn, lima beans, tomatoes and a hearty beef bone. Big Mama's specialty was Delmonico steaks which we call rib eyes these days. Aunt Christine made an out-of-this-world, "sock-it-to-me" box cake with her additions of whipping cream and extra spices to the recipe. She also made super fried chicken.

Lovely Rack of Lamb

Lamb anyone? This recipe calls for a five minute Worcestershire sauce marinade followed by a dusting of garlic and onion powder, a generous sprinkle of sea salt and pepper. Next it's into a hot pan for a hard sear on each side. Then it's into a 450 degree oven for three to five minutes depending on your desired temperature. Enjoy!

It's all in the sear!

GG's Best Rib Eye Steak

Who doesn't enjoy a good steak? This version calls for a ten minute pineapple/Worcestershire sauce marinade with a dusting of garlic and onion powder, a generous sprinkle of sea salt and pepper. Next it's into a hot pan or onto a hot grill pan for a hard sear on each side. Then it's into a 450 degree oven for three to five minutes depending on desired temperature. Enjoy!

Family Style Cornish Hens

These tasty little birds are family favorites. Big Mama served them with traditional stuffing and green beans. Derek, Sr. likes to roast them on the grill. Bernice stuffs them with brown and wild rice. Joshua dresses them with garden herbs. The secret is to cook them until the skin is crispy and the meat is still tender and juicy.

GG's Basic Recipe

2 lbs. Cornish hens (4)
1/4 c. olive oil
2 tsp. salt
2 tsp. white pepper
1 tsp. celery seed
1 tsp. poultry seasoning
1/4 cup fresh rosemary
1/2 c. butter, melted

Optional: Select a stuffing and additional seasonings of your choice. Suggestions: Seasoned crumbled cornbread with raisins moistened with poultry broth; seasoned brown and wild rice; chopped dates and raisins; pineapple or orange sections; garden herbs and vegetables such as onions, celery and carrots. Use pan drippings for sauce or gravy.

Preheat oven to 250*. Prepare hens. Wash and pat dry. Rub with oil. Season inside and outside with seasonings above. Now, this is where your creativity kicks in. Add your preferred seasonings and/or stuffing of your choice. Pour melted butter over hens. Place hens in roasting pan and cook in oven for 35 minutes or until golden brown. Serve with tasty sides. Enjoy!

Savory Smothered Cubed Steak

Smothered gravy variations of proteins are a favorite as far as comfort foods go in the South. This dish works for fried chicken, fried pork chops, and even fried fish. Inspired by Darlene's version of Salisbury Steak this dish is memorable and delicious. You can enjoy rice flour for the gluten shy table. Onions are quite a compliment in this versatile "country fried" dish.

Basic Recipe

1 pound Chopped Cube Steak
¼ cup cooking oil
1 cup rice flour
1 tsp. salt
1 tsp. pepper
1 tsp. garlic powder
¼ cup Worcestershire sauce
1 large yellow onion
1 cup hot water

Optional: This recipe also works well with fried chicken; beef, calf and chicken liver; pork chops; fish; and vegetables such as green tomatoes, eggplant, tofu and jack fruit.

Season cube steak or preferred protein with salt, pepper and garlic powder. Coat with rice flour. Heat oil in hot skillet. Slice or chop onion. Sauté onion in oil until translucent. Remove onion from pan. Add meat to pan, brown on both sides. Remove from pan. Add hot water to drippings remaining in the pan to form a roux. Add additional flour or oil to thicken if needed; add more water if needed for desired consistency. Return meat or veggies to pan, cover with onions. Heat together until gravy bubbles. Serve with sides. Enjoy!

GG's "Sunday Supper Meatloaf"

Basic Ingredients

3 pounds ground meat
6 boiled eggs
2 stalks chopped celery
½ cup arugula
¼ cup fresh rosemary
Sea Salt
Assorted Pepper (optional)
½ cup Mustard or Ketchup
¼ Honey (for turkey)
¼ cup Worcestershire Sauce
Olive oil spray
½ cup olive oil
¼ cup minced garlic
¼ cup minced onion
1 tbs. Smokey paprika
½ cup chopped bell peppers

Preheat oven to 425 degrees. Place meat in a bowl. Combine all ingredients except eggs, mustard or ketchup, honey and arugula. Press out a "bed" for the eggs and arugula. Lay eggs over arugula in the center. Drizzle with ketchup or mustard and honey. Keep remaining for topping. Press the meat over the eggs to make a loaf. Cook in oven until done. (about 30 minutes) Remove from oven, drizzle topping over. Serve with tasty sides. Enjoy!

GG's Traditional Beef Meatloaf with Tomato Sauce

GG's Colorful Spaghetti Surprise

Some of us in the family wanted a tasty alternative to tomato based red pizza and spaghetti sauce. While this was a tall order, it is truly written that "nothing is impossible with God." This tasty sauce is guaranteed to surprise and delight your taste buds.

Basic Ingredients

1 cup olive oil
¼ cup sea salt
5 parsnips
5 carrots
1 cup pickled beets
1 cup chopped celery
2 chopped onions
½ cup minced garlic
½ cup fresh rosemary
½ cup Italian seasoning
1 cup water
Choice of noodles or pasta (including veggie spirals)

Combine all ingredients in a large mixing bowl. Scoop or pour into food processor and blend or puree to desired consistency. (Depending on size of processing bowl, you may have to repeat this step.) Pour the mixture into a pot and bring to a bubbling simmer. Reduce heat and cook until sauce thickens to desired consistency. Meanwhile prepare noodles or pasta. When ready, spoon sauce over them; serve and enjoy!

Burger Ideas

GG's Blue Cheese Burgers

Salmon Burgers

There's always time for a good burger. Pick your protein and build your favorite. I enjoy blue cheese burgers for our parties. For spectacular turkey burgers, Mrs. Audrey adds blueberries.

Turkey Burgers

Yummy Roasted Veggies

Roasted Cabbage

Roasted Parsnip

Roasted okra, garlic & peppers

Sides can be nutritious show stoppers; sure to please the most "picky" palates. Roasted, French fried, steamed, boiled or raw; most veggies are chocked full of fiber and healthy antioxidants. Sacrifice carbs, not taste!

Root vegetables are especially good when roasted in the oven. Yet there is much to be said in favor of variety. We enjoy a medley of assorted veggies; corn, squash, onions, beets and carrots.

After preheating the oven to 425 degrees, we chop the vegetables, place them in a large roasting pan, drizzle coconut oil over them, sprinkle them with sea salt, garlic and our smoky paprika and cook until tender to the touch (about 25 minutes). Enjoy!

GG's "Who Stole the Meat?"

Sautéed Mixed Greens

Looking for a new twist on southern cooking? Try sautéing your favorite greens with oil and vinegar. Collards, kale, turnips and mustard greens can be combined for a hearty blend.

Ingredients: 2 lbs. fresh chopped greens. ¼ cup Vinegar (your choice). Sea Salt to taste. ½ cup olive oil. ¼ cup chopped or minced onion. 2tbs. smoked paprika. 1 cup of water.

Combine all ingredients in a large pot. Stir well. Cook on stovetop on medium setting; stirring occasionally until greens are tender. Enjoy!

GG's Collard Greens and Pasta Surprise

"Where There's a Will, There's a Way

I have a little secret to share. When I discovered that chicken, tomatoes, night shades veggies, and gluten don't agree with my dietary wheel house, I was devastated to say the least. Having cooked with these popular ingredients for decades, I was yet undaunted. The friendly GF substitutes such as rice flour and almond flour add a new dimension of flavor that family and Friends can enjoy as well. It's also Easy to just make two dishes at mealtimes; one traditional and one GF. This way, everyone is happy.

When a request came for GG to make a "non Alfredo, tomato and gluten free yet delicious pasta dish", the challenge was on. This dish surprises happy diners.

Ingredients

1 pound ground turkey	Sea salt to taste
1 cup finely chopped celery	¼ cup chopped onions
1 cup fat free half and half	¼ cup minced garlic
½ cup parmesan cheese	Pinch of rosemary
¼ cup olive oil	1 cup shredded collard greens
¼ cup Italian seasoning	Dash of nutmeg

Brown turkey in olive oil in a pan on stove top. Add celery, onions and garlic, cook until translucent. Add salt, Italian seasoning, nutmeg, rosemary, cheese and half and half. Stir until cheese softens. Stir in collard greens, cook until greens become tender (about three minutes). Plate up and serve. Enjoy!

GG's Demshos and Musgos
(Nice Names for Leftovers)

While compiling the book, realizing that we often have viewpoints, we wondered how to incorporate our faith, our world view, and our life experiences, which are often controversial, into a book about food without giving our readers indigestion. That's when our friend Jerry Van shared some very important insight regarding the purpose of this cookbook: "Everyone has to eat." Amen. And so it is.

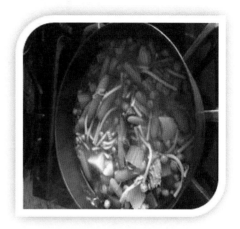

We approach this thought in the section on "leftovers" because, let's face it, everyone has baggage in life. Such is also the case with our edible leftovers. Whether it's that half eaten pizza, that overcooked heel of a delicious roast, a sprouting potato or a scraggly celery stalk.; there's still something worth saving in the stew of life.

Here is a lesson I learned from my mother-in-law during my early years of marriage. She offered me a cooking lesson and words of wisdom at the same time. She was in her tiny kitchen and I was her souse chef. I asked her what she was making, and she said: "Demshos and Musgos." Of course I had never heard of such a thing, so she opened her fridge and pantry doors, and said: "Dem Sunday leftovers sho' must go!"

We made the best pot of stew that I've ever eaten that day. What can we do with a repurposed meal or a repurposed destiny? Food for thought.

Asians have their fried rice from left over rice, veggies and meats. The Irish have their mulligan stew. GG has demshos and musgos. This dish is one of a dozen versions. (Depends on what's left on the shelf.)

Quick and Easy Desert Ideas

Add apples and raisins and extra spices and extracts to your favorite boxed cake mix. Substitute whipping cream for liquids and butter for oil. Bake as directed. Top with whipped cream. Voila!

For a pretty yet quick desert, take leftover pound cake or shortbread cookies and layer with seasonal fruit and whipped cream in a wine glass or punchbowl. Sprinkle with orange zest. Enjoy!

Jan's Delish Carrot Cake

Ingredients

2 cups sugar
2 cups all purpose flour
2 teaspoon baking soda
1 teaspoon salt
1 cup vegetable oil
4 eggs
3 cups grated carrots
2 teaspoon cinnamon
Sprinkle nutmeg and all spice

Frosting

Ingredients

1 (8 oz) package cream cheese, softened
½ cup butter, softened
1 (16 oz) package powdered sugar
1 teaspoon vanilla
1 cup chopped nuts

Sift dry ingredients together into large mixing bowl. Add oil, mixing thoroughly. Add eggs, beating well. Stir in carrots and cinnamon. Pour batter into two 9 inch round baking pans. Bake at 350 degrees for 35 minutes. Cake is very moist; let stand uncovered for about an hour or until cooled. Prepare frosting by blending cream cheese and margarine until smooth. Add sugar and vanilla and beat well. Spread on cooled cake and sprinkle nuts. Serve with ice cream or coffee! Enjoy!

Beverages

GG's Holiday Punch

Basic Ingredients

1 quart grape juice
1 quart lemonade
1 liter ginger ale
1 pint club soda
1 tsp. orange peel
1 quart of pineapple juice
   (optional)
1 sliced lemon or orange

Versions of this punch, inspired by
The Farris Family, have refreshed
our tables for years. Simply pour
all of the ingredients into a spouted
pitcher, stir, serve over crushed ice
and garnish with fresh fruit. Enjoy!

GG's Wassel (Hot Spiced Punch)

Basic Ingredients

1 1/3 cup sugar
1 qt. water
5 whole cloves
4 sticks cinnamon
2 tsp. allspice
3 cups orange juice
1 cup pineapple juice
(optional)
2 cups lemonade
2 qt. apple cider

This drink is especially warm
and comforting for winter
holidays. Simply heat all of the
ingredients together and pour
into a heat supporting urn, and
serve in pretty tea cups. Enjoy!

KIDS COOK TOO!

In our family, we learn to cook early. Often babies in the high chair are given a bowl with cracked eggs and a fork and are guided into the art of whisking eggs for scramble.

Christine, Martin and Alfred (Chris, ML and AD) learned to cook in the now historic family home on Auburn Avenue in Atlanta. Their Grandmother Jenny Parks Williams ruled the kitchen domain; and as youngsters, the trio were test kitchen taste masters who managed to learn some memorable techniques that have been passed down through the generations.

With the onset of children's cooking shows on television and social media, it seems that this section is right on time.

Maryn Makes Peary Applesauce

Maryn with Mommy

Ingredients
6 Apples (2 each; red,
   green, yellow)
1 pear
1 cup organic cane sugar
1 tsp. cinnamon
1 tsp. gingerbread seasoning
Boiling Water

Bring 6 cups of water to boiling. Meanwhile, peel and dice
the pear and apples. Place apples and pear into the boiling
water. Cook until tender and breaking apart with a fork.
Remove from water, drain and put into a blender. Blend until
just chunky, yet smooth enough for a baby to eat. Add spices
and sugar. Stir. Refrigerate to cool off. Serve in pretty cups or
bowls. Enjoy!

Aliscia makes Heavenly Cheese and Eggs

The secret to making delicious scrambled eggs is patience, patience, patience. This young home cook has been making scrumptious eggs since she was four years old! She learned the art from her daddy who is also her souse chef.

Ingredients
6 fresh eggs
Sea Salt to taste
Pepper to taste
¼ stick butter
½ cup cheddar cheese

Heat skillet on medium temperature on stove. Break eggs into a medium sized mixing bowl; be careful not to drop shells into the bowl. Gently stir eggs until yoke blends with egg whites (about two minutes). Melt butter into pan. Pour eggs into pan and gently stir until eggs are fluffy and not dry. Sprinkle salt, pepper and cheese into pan with the eggs and stir for about 30 seconds. Serve with toast, fruit and breakfast bacon. Enjoy!

Friends' and Family "Celeb" Covered Dish Ideas

Oh what fun it is to share favorite holiday recipe ideas with friends and family across the globe. Sometimes, we get pleasant surprises as we discover that many of our celebrated radio/television talk show hosts, preachers, pastors, civil rights warriors, prolife warriors, prayer warriors and other "personalities" that we admire and watch from afar are also great "home cooks." Again, we may not all agree on policy, but we breathe the same air; and we all have to eat!

We've included in this section dishes inspired by some of our friends who like to share recipe ideas from their kitchens. Some of my fondest moments have been spent with sharing conversations about food and life with friends such as Jerry Horn and Chris. Often, it starts with "how do you make your…" Before it's all over, we forget politics, our favorite sports team, what's happening on the news, and we are just enjoying the finer things of life, including ideas for making good food for our families and friends.

Mr. Rodney's Greens   **Sister Bennett's Sorrel**   **Chris' Holiday Cake**

Mrs. Audrey Sets the Tone & Table

This cookbook blossomed from our "Home for the Holidays" video which was recorded by Jan Horne. Our set designer was Mrs. Audrey Fields. She is a wonderful professional event planner. Her staging of the decorations, table designs, floral arrangements and her stunning hors d'oeuvres were such an inspiration that we thought you'd enjoy meeting her.

GG's Quick and Tasty Tangy Salad Dressing

Ingredients
½ cup olive oil
2 tbs. fresh lemon juice
½ tbs. Dijon mustard
Dash of ginger
1 tbs. honey
Pinch Himalayan salt and white pepper

Optional
Substitute white balsamic vinegar for the lemon juice.

Stir, mix or shake ingredients together and pour over your favorite salad bowl. Enjoy!

100 Layers of Nacre – The Making of a Pearl
The Parable of the Pearl of Great Price

Michelle Uchiyama
"One Woman's Journey"

Edited by Evangelist Alveda C. King
Foreword by Prophetess Connie Williams

"Again, the kingdom of heaven is like a merchant seeking beautiful pearls, who, when he had found one pearl of great price, went and sold all that he had and bought it. Matthew 13:45-46

Michelle left Planet Earth headed for Heaven in 2017. Yet, I still remember her brilliance in everything; including the kitchen. One day, a few years ago, we were having a business brunch; combination "Lunch and Learn" and networking at my house. Wouldn't you know it; all the salad dressing in the frig was expired. "Shelly Dear" to the rescue. "No worries," she said. "Let's make some now." And we did, with what was on hand. Good thing our frig and pantry were well stocked.

Kolachy (GF)

Ingredients

½ cup rice flour
½ cup almond flour
1 stick softened butter (or oil substitute)
Dash of Orange Peel
3 oz cream cheese
1 cup Real fruit jam or jelly (your choice)

Preheat oven to 400 degrees. Combine all ingredients in a bowl. Mix until dough can form a solid yet soft ball. Refrigerate for one hour. Remove from refrigerator. Form dough into a ball the size of a silver dollar. Lay the cookies on a greased or nonstick baking sheet. Press each center with the back of a teaspoon or your thumb. Stir the orange peel into the jelly and spoon into the center of each cookie. Bake until firm; as the jelly just begins to bubble remove from oven, allow to cool thoroughly. Enjoy!

Diane and Ruth are my publicists. We travel, a LOT. On the road we talk about how we miss our families and can't wait till we get back home to them, and our gardens and kitchens. I heard about these cookies from them, and combined the concept with my thumbprint cookie recipe. Have fun with this festive treat.

Weddings are Holidays Too!

Frappe Punch is a favorite wedding punch in our family. Frappe is also popular at church socials. This frothy beverage is made with your favorite ice cream and or sherbet or sorbet and combined over ice with juice and a carbonated soda. Pray over the marriages and enjoy the festivities!

AD and Naomi

ML and Coretta

Alveda with Daddy

Eddie and LaShundra

Kitchen Glossary

Mrs. Naomi Ruth Barber King, the Butterfly Queen is also known as a famous "shake and pour" cook. This section is a tribute to her and her mother "Big Mama" Bessie Barber Bailey.

Dash – one shake from a bottle or jar.

Pinch – as much as you can grasp Between your thumb and forefinger.
Firm to touch – using a finger to test Doneness

Umami – a relatively new term for home cooks that describes a savory dish, with the flavor often uniquely found in a particular culture or Chef's cooking style.

Make you wanna' slap yo' Mama – a food dish so good that you want to do this. Not recommended that you try it though.

Dem Shos and Musgoes – Dem (them/those) leftovers Sho (sure) must go.

Farm to Table – another phrase for organic. Made from Scratch – prepared without using packaged or canned ingredients.

Alveda C. King is a Christian evangelist and civil rights activist and is also known for her creative contributions in film, music, politics, education and journalism. She is also an actress, singer, songwriter, blogger, author (including KING TRUTHS, AMERICA RETURN TO GOD, KING RULES, WHO WE ARE IN CHRIST JESUS), FOX NEWS Contributor and a television and radio personality.

As a former GA State Legislator, Director of Civil Rights for the Unborn for Priests for Life, and devoted mother and grandmother, she is also a guardian of the King Family Legacy. Alveda is the daughter of Rev. A. D. King and Mrs. Naomi King, the granddaughter of Rev. Martin Luther King, Sr. and Mrs. Alberta Williams King, and the niece of Dr. Martin Luther King, Jr.

Jan has been creating videos since 1996. Shortly after that started Studio 25 Productions. Some of her corporate clients have included the University of Georgia, Siemens Airfield Solutions, Rainbow Vacuum Cleaners, the Hansberger Group, Delta Air Lines and Honda Corporation, to name a few. In 2004 she began working for a local access channel producing six programs weekly and later producing the East Coweta High School Football show. Besides corporate production, since 1999, she has been creating cinematic style wedding movies that are entertaining and fun to watch. In addition Studio 25 Productions creates political videos. She is also actively involved in numerous local and national associations.

Index

Kitchen Notes:

Kitchen Notes:

Kitchen Notes:

94071090R00031